Service is the rent we pay for the privilege of living on this earth.

...a woman in the whitehouse... **SHIRLEY!**

You make progress by implementing ideas.

For my mother, Oscie, who taught me
my voice mattered from the start.
—T.F.B.

To Marietta. Thank you for just the
right words at just the right time.
—N.C.

not done yet

Shirley Chisholm's Fight for Change

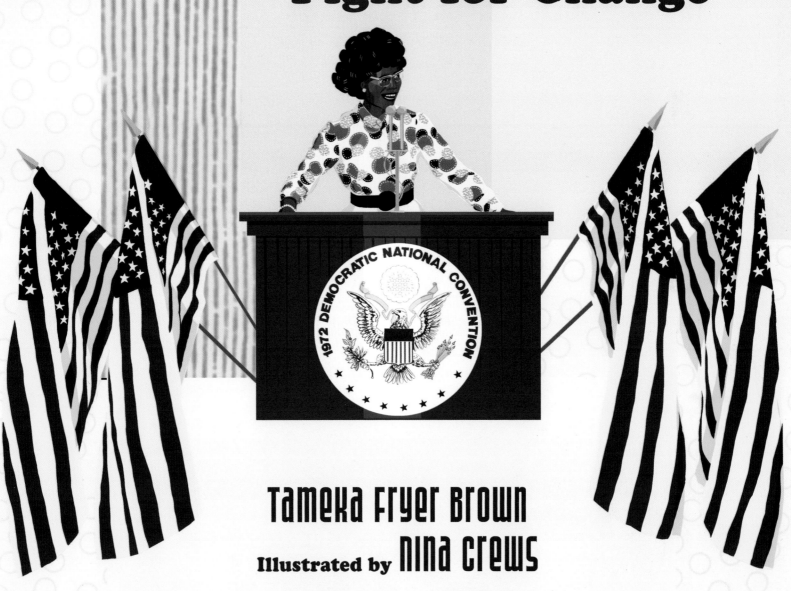

Tameka Fryer Brown
Illustrated by Nina Crews

M Millbrook Press / Minneapolis

Before she was born, Shirley
would kick so hard,
her mother knew she was aching
to come out and fight.

Her mother was right.
Shirley Chisholm was a natural-born fighter.
She didn't like to be bossed
and she wanted things to be fair.

Little Shirley and her sisters
went to live
on Grandmother's farm in Barbados.
Life was rich with sweet breadfruit, cassava, and yams,
sunny people,
and the bluest Caribbean Sea.

After six years, Mother took them back
to cold, crowded, confusing Brooklyn.
It was a struggle,
but Shirley finally learned to love it too.

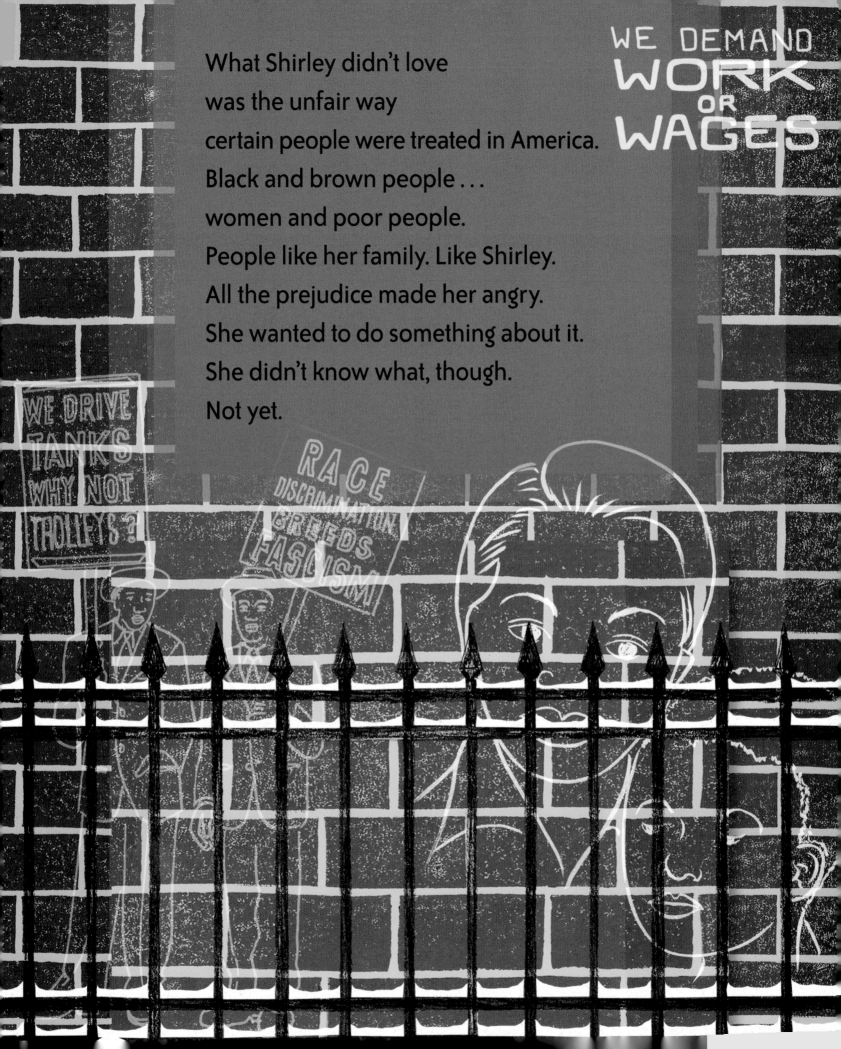

What Shirley didn't love

was the unfair way

certain people were treated in America.

Black and brown people . . .

women and poor people.

People like her family. Like Shirley.

All the prejudice made her angry.

She wanted to do something about it.

She didn't know what, though.

Not yet.

Shirley and her sisters excelled in school
because Mother and Papa expected it.
Study. Make something of yourselves,
Papa said.
Shirley took his message to heart.

If school and learning
could make *her* life better,
they could also be Shirley's destiny.
**I'll help lift others by
becoming a teacher.**
And she did,
but destiny had more in mind.

Shirley got involved
in a Brooklyn political club.
The women in the club worked hard to earn money
that only the men got to use.

This isn't fair, Shirley said to the club.
We raised it.
We should get to use it too!

Shirley is right!
The women backed her up.
The men had no choice but to share.
She showed speaking out
could make a real difference.
She was proud,
but she wasn't done yet.

For years,
Shirley worked night and day
for leaders she thought would help Brooklyn.
After a while, she began to believe
the best person to lead might be . . .

Shirley.

Shirley entered the race
to represent Brooklyn
in the New York State Assembly.
When neighbors told her women
should not run for office,
she made them all a promise:

Fighting Shirley Chisholm
will always fight for you.

Enough of them believed her and she won!
She was Brooklyn's first Black assemblywoman.
A great triumph—
but she wasn't done yet.

Assemblywoman Chisholm got straight to work speaking up for the poor and ignored.

The men in the assembly didn't like her style.
Little lady—you should be more quiet.

Instead,

she spoke louder

and worked even harder.

Eight bills she wrote became laws.

She was keeping her promise, but she wanted to do more . . .

. . . so she ran for the United States Congress.

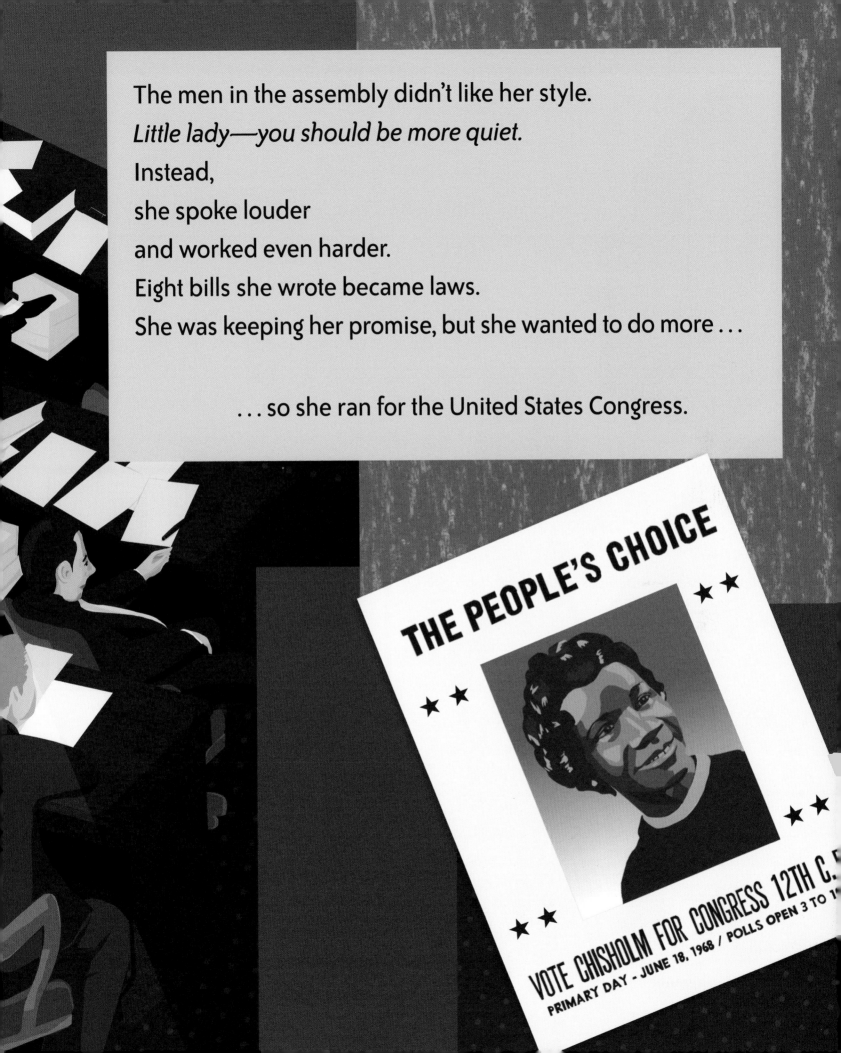

It was a difficult battle from the start.

In using her voice for change,
it seemed
Shirley had made many enemies.
They mocked her
and did everything they could
to make sure that she would lose.

A little schoolteacher can't lead us, they said.
What we need is a big, strong man.

This made women furious!

Show them with your vote,

Shirley said.

They did . . . and she won!

The first Black woman ever elected to Congress!

She made history!

But she wasn't done yet.

When Representative Chisholm
walked the hallowed halls of Congress,
the thing she felt most
was unwelcome.

No one would sit with her at lunch.
Her colleagues made nasty remarks.
One man even spat when she entered the room.
All to scare her
and keep her in her place.

As usual, Shirley didn't back down.
She stayed focused
on what she'd come to do.
She hired a staff of all women.
She fiercely demanded rights for all.
She fought for the environment,
for children, for health care.

A righteous rebel who earned respect,
she made her mark.
But she wasn't done yet.

Shirley championed bold ideas
to better the country she loved.
But how could she get more people to listen?

FRI., JAN., 14
at 8 p.m.

L.A. Convention
Center

$1 DONATION

I know . . .
I'll run for president.

No Black person
or woman had seriously
run for president before.
But Shirley was serious.
She wanted to win,
to show others they could win too.

Shirley traveled the country
sharing her vision
of liberty and justice for all.

Let us move beyond hate so America works for the neglected, the forgotten, for everyone.

Shirley didn't win.
But the path that she paved
makes a better nation possible
today.

Shirley Chisholm was a natural-born fighter.
She battled for fairness and change.

Her legacy lives.
The fight continues.

We're not done yet.

AUTHOR'S NOTE

Shirley Chisholm reminds me a lot of my grandmother. While Mrs. Chisholm was a highly educated scholar from the North and my southern grandmother's formal education ended after the eighth grade, both were strong women who weren't afraid to stand up for what they believed was right, even when it meant standing alone. They both had easy smiles, sharp tongues, and a low tolerance for nonsense. They were also close in age, born only eleven months apart. These similarities motivated me to write about Congresswoman Chisholm, and they also shaped the way I chose to tell her story.

She was born Shirley Anita St. Hill in Brooklyn, New York, but still considered herself a "Bajan girl." She lived on her grandmother's farm in Christ Church, Barbados, from the ages of three to nine—years she believed pivotal in shaping her personality. Her West Indian parents, Charles and Ruby St. Hill, had taken Shirley and her sisters to live there so they could work extra jobs and earn enough money to comfortably care for the entire family. Mrs. Chisholm attributed much of her self-esteem and success in life to those years in Barbados; in particular, she felt the farm-life chores, the spiritual foundation, and the high expectations of her family and teachers were crucial to her development. I personally identify with this part of her story because I, too, am a person of strong faith who grew up with family members and teachers who encouraged me to always do and be my best.

Young Shirley acquired her father's passion for current events, politics, and a good intellectual debate. Her mother took her and her sisters to the library every two weeks to check out books, which they discussed at the dinner table. Thanks to her family's focus on education, Shirley graduated from Girls' High School near the top of her class, Brooklyn College with honors, and Columbia University with a master's degree in early childhood education. She also played piano, loved to dance, was great at impressions, and spoke fluent Spanish.

As an activist-politician, Mrs. Chisholm was known as Fighting Shirley Chisholm because she continually challenged those in power to make decisions that were fair and just. She called herself "unbought and unbossed" because she refused to be influenced by money or fear in her fight for equity.

What people remember most about Shirley Chisholm are her "firsts." But those aren't what she most wanted to be remembered for. In an interview with documentarian Shola Lynch, Mrs. Chisholm said, "When I die, I want to be remembered as a woman who lived in the twentieth century and who dared to be a catalyst for change. I don't want to be remembered as the first Black woman who went to Congress. And I don't even want to be remembered as the first woman who happened to be Black to make a bid for the Presidency. I want to be remembered as a woman who fought for change in the twentieth century. That's what I want."

FIGHTING SHIRLEY CHISHOLM. A CATALYST FOR CHANGE. That's how I'll remember her. I hope you will too.

Illustrator's Note

I feel I have always known of Shirley Chisholm, though I find it impossible to recall when I first heard her name. I grew up in New York City in the 1960s and 1970s, so it makes sense that she was familiar to me. I've always thought of her as an icon of feminist strength and Black pride. Illustrating this book has taught me so much more about her. I knew she was brilliant, and I now understand how she used her brilliance strategically to make a difference in Congress. I knew she was bold, and I now see that her certainty came both from deep inside herself and from the love and support of people close to her. I knew she was one of the first women to run for president of the United States. Now I know that she was also a teacher and a big sister.

When I began working on the illustrations, I read Chisholm's autobiography to better imagine her childhood. I studied videos and photos of her many years in public life. I fell in love with her sense of style and her wigs. I noted the playful look in her eyes and the confidence of her stride. Tameka Fryer Brown's words capture Chisholm's energy and drive perfectly. I used bold colors and layered shapes in my illustrations to keep that energy going. I wanted the reader to feel that they were in Chisholm's world, so I emphasized the patterns of her clothes by repeating those patterns in the backgrounds of the illustrations. I surrounded her with people, because her deep commitment to people made her the leader that she was. I loved getting to know Shirley Chisholm through working on this book. I hope you enjoy getting to know her too.

CHISHOLM

UNBOUGHT AND UNBOSSED

TIMELINE

1924 On November 30, Shirley Anita St. Hill is born in Brooklyn, New York, to Charles and Ruby (Seale) St. Hill, West Indian immigrants from British Guiana and Barbados. Shirley is the firstborn of four daughters.

1928–1934 Shirley and her sisters Odessa and Muriel live on their maternal grandmother's farm in Barbados. Early in 1928, Ruby leaves the girls with her mother, Emaline (Emily) Seale, while she and Charles work extra jobs to save up money for a house and their daughters' college educations. In March of 1934, Ruby takes Shirley, Odessa, and Muriel back to Brooklyn. Because of the Great Depression, she and Charles still haven't saved any money, but they miss their girls and want their family back together again. A fourth daughter, Selma, is born while the other girls are still in Barbados.

1942 Shirley graduates from Girls' High School with several college scholarship offers. Her family cannot afford the boarding costs of an out-of-town school, so she decides to attend nearby Brooklyn College.

1946 Shirley graduates cum laude from Brooklyn College, with a bachelor's degree in sociology and a minor in Spanish. While there, she joined the Harriet Tubman Society and the debate team, cofounded a Black women's student society called Ipothia (In Pursuit of the Highest in All), and began her foray into politics by joining the Seventeenth Assembly District (17AD) Democratic Club in Bedford-Stuyvesant.

Shirley is hired as a teacher's aide at Mount Calvary Child Care Center in Harlem, New York. She is later promoted to teacher and works there for seven years.

1949 Shirley St. Hill marries Conrad Chisholm, a private investigator originally from Jamaica, in a big West Indian wedding.

1951 Shirley graduates with a master's degree in early childhood education (Curriculum and Teaching) from Columbia University's Teachers College.

1953 Shirley becomes director of the Friend in Need Nursery School in Brooklyn, New York.

1954 Shirley accepts the directorship of the Hamilton-Madison Childcare Center in Manhattan, supervising a staff of twenty-four and responsible for the care of 130 children, aged three to seven.

Shirley is one of the founding organizers of the Bedford-Stuyvesant Political League (BSPL), an "insurgent political club" created to get more Black people elected to public office.

1958 Shirley decides to run for BSPL president against Wesley (Mac) Holder, her mentor who has been president since the club was founded. This causes a long-lasting rift between the two. When Mac is reelected, Shirley leaves the BSPL, the 17AD Democratic Club, and politics altogether.

1959 Shirley becomes a consultant to the New York City Division of Day Care, supervising ten center directors, evaluating programs and curricula, and setting childcare standards for the entire city.

1960 Shirley is one of six cofounders of the Unity Democratic Club, whose goal is to get more Black and Puerto Rican people elected to public office in the Seventeenth District.

1964 Shirley wins her first political race and becomes the first Black woman to represent Brooklyn in the New York State Assembly.

1965–1968 Shirley represents Brooklyn's Seventeenth District in New York's State Assembly. She is very active on behalf of her constituents, introducing fifty bills—eight of which become laws—addressing needs such as unemployment insurance for domestic and agricultural workers, childcare for the working poor, and a program called SEEK that provides academic, financial, and social support to students who might not otherwise be able to attend college.

1966 Shirley becomes a member of the newly founded National Organization for Women (NOW).

1968 Shirley enters the race to become a member of the United States Congress. Her campaign slogan is Fighting Shirley Chisholm: Unbought and Unbossed. With the support of the women in her district (and her former mentor, Mac Holder), Shirley wins!

1969 Shirley arrives in Washington, DC, to represent the Twelfth Congressional District in the United States House of Representatives. She is the first Black woman ever elected to Congress. Right away, she uses her platform to speak out against the Vietnam War and challenges a committee assignment she doesn't believe will help her serve the people of Brooklyn.

Shirley is initiated into the Brooklyn Alumnae Chapter of Delta Sigma Theta Sorority, Incorporated.

1970 Shirley publishes her autobiography, *Unbought and Unbossed*.

1971 Shirley is a founding member of the Congressional Black Caucus.

Shirley is a founding member of the National Women's Political Caucus.

1972 On January 25, Shirley invites voters to join her "on the Chisholm Trail" as she announces her decision to seek the Democratic nomination for president at Concord Baptist Church in Brooklyn. She is the first African American and the first woman to make a serious bid for the nomination and office.

Shirley ultimately amasses 152 delegates and finishes in fourth place at the Democratic National Convention. George McGovern becomes the Democratic Party nominee for president of the United States. He is defeated by Richard Nixon in the general election.

1973 Shirley publishes her second book, *The Good Fight*.

1977 Shirley becomes the first Black congresswoman to serve on the powerful House Rules Committee.

Shirley's divorce with Conrad Chisholm becomes final in February. She marries Arthur Hardwick Jr. in November.

1983 Congresswoman Shirley Anita Chisholm retires from the US House of Representatives. During her seven terms in office, she consistently fought for underserved and oppressed communities, especially in the areas of education, health care, environmental protections, women's rights, civil rights, and voting rights.

1983–1987 Shirley is a professor at Mount Holyoke College, teaching courses in sociology, politics, and women's studies.

1984 Shirley is cofounder of the National Congress of Black Women.

1985 Shirley is a visiting scholar at Spelman College.

Shirley is honored with the Distinguished Achievement medal from Columbia University's Teachers College.

1993 Shirley is nominated to be US ambassador to Jamaica by President Bill Clinton, but she declines the nomination due to poor health.

Shirley is inducted into the National Women's Hall of Fame.

2005 On January 1, Shirley Chisholm dies in Ormond Beach, Florida, at the age of eighty.

2006 On June 5, documentarian Shola Lynch accepts a 2005 Peabody Award for *Chisholm '72: Unbought & Unbossed*, a documentary about Shirley's historic presidential campaign.

2015 On November 24, Shirley Chisholm is posthumously awarded the Presidential Medal of Freedom—the highest civilian honor in the United States of America—by President Barack Obama.

2019 On July 2, the 407-acre (165 ha) Shirley Chisholm State Park opens in Brooklyn, New York.

2020 On November 30, Vice President–elect Kamala Harris honors the birthday of Congresswoman Chisholm with the following words: "Unbought and unbossed, Shirley Chisholm paved the way for me and so many others. On her birthday, we celebrate her brilliance and boldness to break down barriers, fight to increase the minimum wage, and speak for those who otherwise wouldn't have a voice in the political process."

Selected Bibliography

Chisholm, Shirley. *Unbought and Unbossed: Expanded 40th Anniversary Edition.* Washington, DC: Take Root Media, 2010.

"CHISHOLM, Shirley Anita." US House of Representatives, History, Art & Archives. Accessed March 10, 2022. https://history.house.gov/People/Listing/C/CHISHOLM,-Shirley-Anita-(C000371)/.

"Conversation with Shirley A. Chisholm (Talking Leadership Series)." YouTube video, 26:25. Posted by Center for American Women and Politics, December 19, 2014. https://www.youtube.com/watch?v=bQPc8EMNFXE.

Lynch, Shola, dir. *Chisholm '72: Unbought & Unbossed.* Beverly Hills, CA: 20th Century Fox Home Entertainment, 2004.

"Shirley Chisholm, Oral History." *Shirley Chisholm: Visionary Videos: NVLP: African American History*, National Visionary Leadership Project, May 7, 2002. http://www.visionaryproject.com/chisholmshirley.

"Shirley Chisholm: Declares Presidential Bid, January 25, 1972." YouTube video, 14:07. Posted by NYC Department of Records and Information Services, April 13, 2015. https://www.youtube.com/watch?v=y3JCX3WxBik.

Winslow, Barbara. *Shirley Chisholm: Catalyst for Change, 1926–2005.* Boulder, CO: Westview, 2014.

Additional Resources

"I'm Just a Bill"—School House Rock
https://www.youtube.com/watch?v=SZ8psP4S6BQ
This classic animated clip describes the process of how a bill becomes a law.

"New York Illustrated: The Irrepressible Shirley Chisholm (1969 NBC News Special)"
https://www.youtube.com/watch?v=ERGWEG4Lcpl
This 1969 profile from NBC News highlights the career and accomplishments of Shirley Chisholm, featuring lots of footage of her speaking and working in Washington, DC.

The Shirley Chisholm Project
http://chisholmproject.com
This website includes a wealth of information about Shirley Chisholm, including materials about Chisholm and other women activists that are part of the Brooklyn College collection.

A Note about Quotations

Shirley Chisholm was a powerful, eloquent speaker. In writing her story as a narrative free verse poem, I made the decision to paraphrase her statements, and those of others, to maintain poetic form and ensure the text would be accessible to young readers. Statements in the main text are all based on things Chisholm said or recounted. The sources for these statements are included in the selected bibliography. Statements on the endsheets and back cover are exact quotes of hers. For more specific source notes, visit my website: www.tamekafryerbrown.com.

Millbrook Press™
An imprint of Lerner Publishing Group, Inc.
241 First Avenue North
Minneapolis, MN 55401 USA

For reading levels and more information, look up this title at www.lernerbooks.com.

Designed by Danielle Carnito and Nina Crews.
Main body text set in Bailey Sans ITC Std. Typeface provided by International Typeface Corporation.
The illustrations in this book were created in Adobe Photoshop using dozens of layers and both digital and handmade patterns and textures.

Library of Congress Cataloging-in-Publication Data

Names: Brown, Tameka Fryer, author. | Crews, Nina, illustrator.
Title: Not done yet : Shirley Chisholm's fight for change / Tameka Fryer Brown ; illustrated by Nina Crews.
Other titles: Shirley Chisholm's fight for change
Description: Minneapolis : Millbrook Press, [2022] | Includes bibliographical references. | Audience: Ages 5–10 | Audience: Grades 2–3 | Summary: "Stirring free verse chronicles Shirley Chisholm's fight for fairness and change on her journey to becoming the first Black woman ever elected to Congress and, in 1972, the first woman to seriously run for president" —Provided by publisher.
Identifiers: LCCN 2021052061 (print) | LCCN 2021052062 (ebook) | ISBN 9781728420080 (library binding) | ISBN 9781728462639 (ebook)
Subjects: LCSH: Chisholm, Shirley, 1924-2005—Juvenile literature. | United States. Congress. House—Biography—Juvenile literature. | African American legislators—Biography—Juvenile literature. | Women legislators—United States—Biography—Juvenile literature. | Legislators—United States—Biography—Juvenile literature. | African American presidential candidates—Biography—Juvenile literature. | Women presidential candidates—United States—Biography—Juvenile literature. | Presidential candidates—United States—Biography—Juvenile literature. | Brooklyn (New York, N.Y.)—Biography—Juvenile literature. | New York (N.Y.)—Biography—Juvenile literature.
Classification: LCC E840.8.C48 B68 2022 (print) | LCC E840.8.C48 (ebook) | DDC 328.73/092 [B]—dc23/eng/20211027

LC record available at https://lccn.loc.gov/2021052061
LC ebook record available at https://lccn.loc.gov/2021052062

Manufactured in the United States of America
1-49119-49288-3/28/2022

MS.CHIS.
FOR
PRES.

Listen to the voice inside yourself that says, I CAN.